MW00975449

L is For Listen
Life Lessons from A to Z

Copyright © 2022 Author Je'Quita Zachary Johnson Written by Je'Quita Zachary Johnson

This Book
Belongs To:

_____

_____

_____

Ask questions.

A B C D E F G H I J K L M N

A to Z
Favorites About Me

Academic Subject

_____

Book

_____

Color

_____

Day

_____

Educator

_____

Food

_____

Gift (given or received)

_____

Hobby

_____

Ice Cream

_____

Joke

_____

Kind Thing to Do for Others

_____

Lady

_____

Man

_____

O P Q R S T U V W X Y Z A B C

Q R S T U V W X Y Z A B C D E

D E F G H I J K L M N O P Q

A to Z
Favorites About Me

Number

_____

Object

_____

Place to Be

_____

Quote

_____

Restaurant

_____

Season

_____

TV Show

_____

Uniform

_____

Video (music or game)

_____

Way to Spend the Day

_____

Xeroxed Memory

_____

Young Person

_____

Zoo Animal

_____

Believe in yourself.

My Goals

Write Your Goals Inside the Target

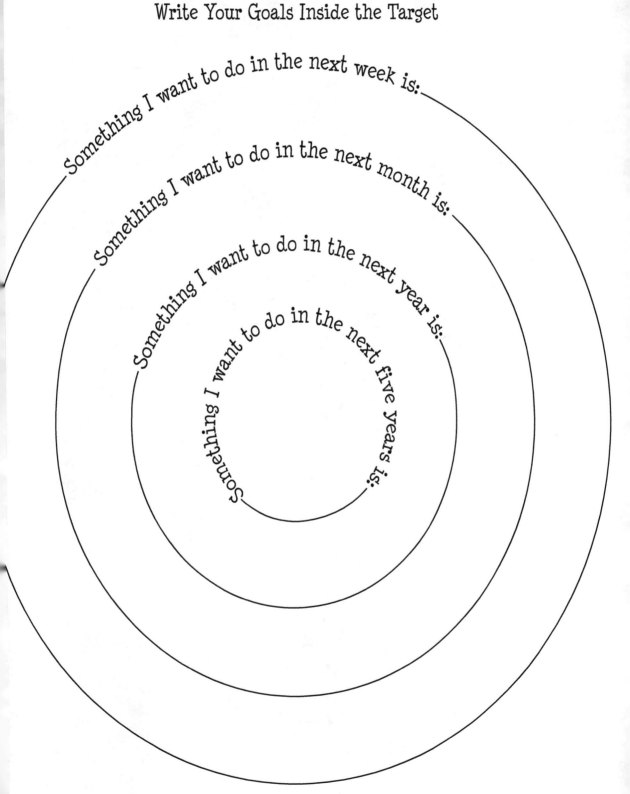

Something I want to do in the next week is:

Something I want to do in the next month is:

Something I want to do in the next year is:

Something I want to do in the next five years is:

Celebrate your achievements.

Road to Success

Write down each success you've had for each phase listed.

1. The Date You Were Born
2. Kindergarten
3. Happy Memories or Events
4. Unhappy or Sad Events

5. New Things You've Learned
6. Successful Things That Have Happened
7. Fun or Exciting Memories
8. Friends You've Made

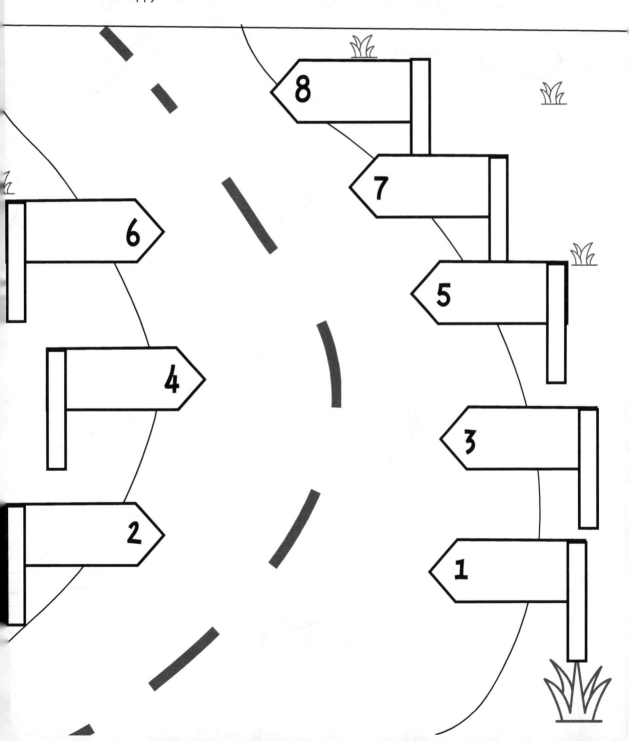

Don't worry.

Color by Word

Color the picture according to the code.

Success	Growth	Advance	Benefit
Orange	Aqua	Green	Yellow
Achievement	Fame	Happiness	Gain
Pink	Purple	Blue	Red

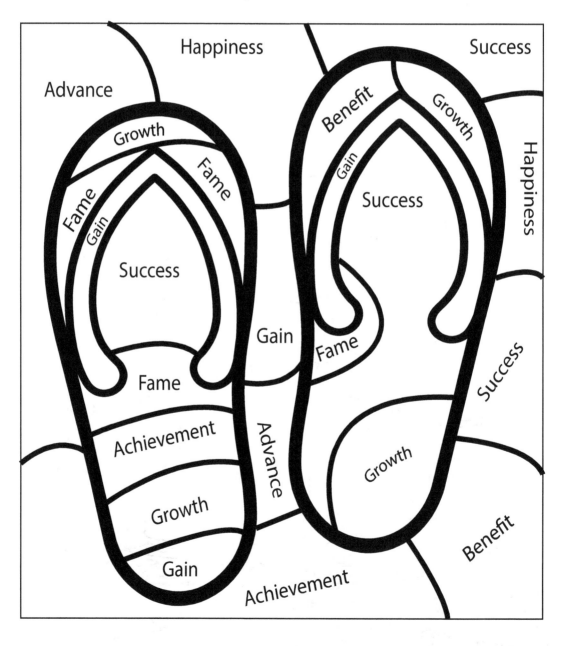

Follow your dreams.

Go for it!

I Can Be Anything

N	A	S	T	E	A	C	H	E	R	E	N	V	I
W	H	M	I	N	I	S	T	E	R	I	E	N	S
K	O	O	A	R	C	H	I	T	E	C	T	L	B
R	R	A	L	I	E	S	N	O	E	E	N	T	A
T	G	V	E	T	E	R	I	N	A	R	I	A	N
E	E	C	O	U	N	S	E	L	O	R	I	R	K
S	R	O	O	E	R	L	V	W	R	K	L	N	T
B	U	S	I	N	E	S	S	O	W	N	E	R	E
T	C	N	E	E	C	R	O	T	L	A	E	R	L
P	O	L	I	C	E	O	F	F	I	C	E	R	L
J	O	E	N	G	I	N	E	E	R	N	E	H	E
R	R	E	R	Z	O	O	L	O	G	I	S	T	R
P	R	O	T	A	R	T	S	U	L	L	I	N	O
J	U	D	G	E	G	A	O	R	E	T	E	R	N

BUSINESS OWNER
POLICE OFFICER
ENGINEER
REALTOR
TEACHER
COUNSELOR
VETERINARIAN
ILLUSTRATOR
JUDGE
ARCHITECT
BANK TELLER
ZOOLOGIST
MINISTER

Journal

Use the prompts to write your thoughts.

I enjoy

_____

_____

_____

I wish

_____

_____

_____

I believe that

_____

_____

_____

I hope that

_____

_____

_____

Journal

Use the prompts to write your thoughts.

I'm looking forward to

_____

_____

_____

The 3 things I love most about my life are

_____

_____

_____

I feel good about myself when

_____

_____

_____

I look good when

_____

_____

_____

Journal

Use the prompts to write your thoughts.

If my mirror could speak, it would say

_____

_____

_____

I love when

_____

_____

_____

The best part of being me is

_____

_____

_____

Handle your business.

Initiate friendships.

Best Friends

Draw a picture of you and a friend.

Motivational Unscramble

Unscramble the tiles to reveal the message.

| doing | You | awesome! | are |

Answer: _____

_____

| tough, | This | but | is | tougher. | you're |

Answer: _____

_____

| stress. | You | Don't | got | this! |

Answer: _____

_____

I'm | making | big | so | and | you! | of

You're | a | change | proud

Answer: _____

_____

good | some | happy | way. | thoughts

Sending | vibes | and | your

Answer: _____

_____

you! | believe | I | in

Answer: _____

_____

| yourself. | good | to | Be |

Answer:_____

_____

| journey | A | step. | one | with | starts |

Answer:_____

_____

| you | than | realize. | braver | You | are |

Answer:_____

_____

Keep moving forward.

Maze

Solve the maze to reach from the word 'life' to the word 'success'.

(Begin here) Life

Success!

Listen.

Make each day great.

Never give up.

Visual Perception

Color the arrows related to their direction.

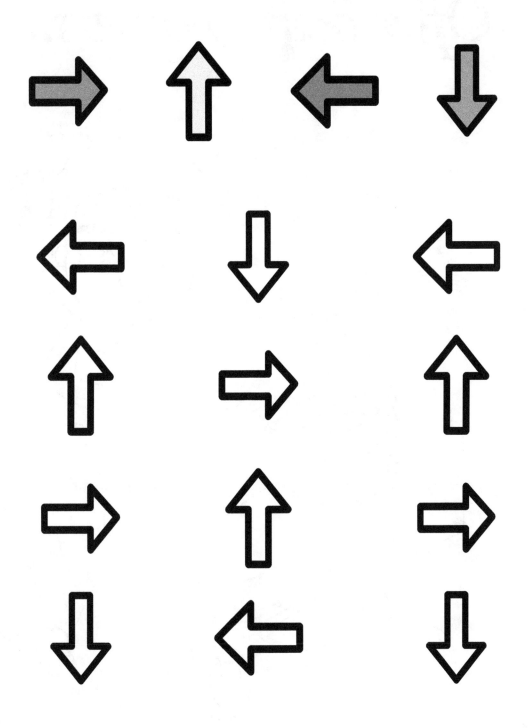

Offer help to others.

Offer to Help Others

Put a check next to each one as you complete it.

☐ Smile and say hello to someone.

☐ Pick up some trash without being asked.

☐ Eat with someone who may be sitting alone in the lunchroom.

☐ Share.

☐ Play with someone new.

☐ Tell someone about the good job they are doing.

☐ Write someone a letter.

☐ Make a picture for someone.

☐ Help clean up even if you did not make the mess.

☐ Donate some clothes.

Practice Patience.

Quench your thirst for knowledge.

Draw a picture
of yourself

Read.

Books

Time to read books and write about them.

Book Title: _____

Author: _____

What was the theme or message from the story?

_____

_____

_____

_____

_____

_____

_____

Books

Time to read books and write about them.

Book Title: _____

Author: _____

What was the theme or message from the story?

_____

_____

_____

_____

_____

_____

_____

Books

Time to read books and write about them.

Book Title: _____

Author: _____

What was the theme or message from the story?

_____

_____

_____

_____

_____

_____

_____

Books

Time to read books and write about them.

Book Title: _____

Author: _____

What was the theme or message from the story?

_____

_____

_____

_____

_____

_____

_____

Books

Time to read books and write about them.

Book Title: _____

Author: _____

What was the theme or message from the story?

_____

_____

_____

_____

_____

_____

_____

Books

Time to read books and write about them.

Book Title: _____

Author: _____

What was the theme or message from the story?

_____

_____

_____

_____

_____

_____

_____

Show love.

Draw a picture
of your family

Gratitude

Gratitude means being thankful for something or someone
and you show it. What are you grateful for?

Date: _____

Today, I am grateful for

_____

_____

_____

I showed I was grateful by

_____

_____

_____

Gratitude

Gratitude means being thankful for something or someone and you show it. What are you grateful for?

Date: _____

Today, I am grateful for

_____

_____

_____

I showed I was grateful by

_____

_____

_____

Gratitude

Gratitude means being thankful for something or someone and you show it. What are you grateful for?

Date: _____

Today, I am grateful for

_____

_____

_____

I showed I was grateful by

_____

_____

_____

Gratitude

Gratitude means being thankful for something or someone and you show it. What are you grateful for?

Date: _____

Today, I am grateful for

_____

_____

_____

I showed I was grateful by

_____

_____

_____

Tell the truth.

Understand directions.

Coloring

Color the picture below by following the directions.

1 - Color the train engine red.

2 - Color two balloons blue.

3 - Color two balloons yellow.

4 - Color the girl with the hat's hair brown.

5 - Color the boy's hat purple.

6 - Color the train cars green.

7 - Draw a train track.

8 - Draw a train station building.

9 - Draw a tree.

10 - Color the rest of the picture.

Value people in your life.

Treasure People in Your Life

People in our lives are a treasure. Write a thank-you note
to someone special in your life.

Treasure

To

Thank you for

Treasure People in Your Life

People in our lives are a treasure. Write a thank-you note to someone special in your life.

Treasure

To

Thank you for

Treasure People in Your Life

People in our lives are a treasure. Write a thank-you note
to someone special in your life.

Treasure

To

Thank you for

Treasure People in Your Life

People in our lives are a treasure. Write a thank-you note
to someone special in your life.

Work hard.

X out fear and doubt.

Draw a picture
of yourself

My Goals for _____

Fill in the blanks below with your goals for the year.

New things I will try this year:

I will learn how to:

I want to be better at:

I will read:

Yield and think
before you speak.

Zip your lips if you don't have anything good to say.

Hey guy, yes! I profess you will be a success!

CPSIA information can be obtained
at www.ICGtesting.com
Printed in the USA
JSHW012031100223
37568JS00003B/30